Stand Up: Bullying Prevention

- Social studies nonfiction about social issues students face and deal with that meets students' need for complex informational text

- Provides realistic advice for dealing with and preventing bullying

- An excellent guidance series to use in an antibullying curriculum

- Explores the role technology plays in bullying

"In this worthwhile series, all types of bullies are exposed. While the battle against bullying has long existed, forms of bullying have evolved to encompass not only physical, but verbal and online as well. ... Are You a Bully? is especially noteworthy, as many bullies don't even realize that they are bullies. Bully-free schools are highlighted; the section on self-esteem is a helpful addition. In an age where bullying has become commonplace, this series is thought-provoking and relevant."
— *Library Media Connection*

School & Library Price reflects 25% off the List Price

Library-bound Book	List $23.60 / S&L	**$17.70**
eBook	List $23.60 / S&L	**$17.70**
Interactive eBook	List $33.25 / S&L	**$24.95**
6-Book Print Set NEW	List $141.60 / S&L **$106.20**	978-1-4777-6632-3

TITLE	DEWEY	GRL/LEXILE	©
Antibullying Clubs Addy Ferguson • 978-1-4777-6631-6 eBook: 978-1-4777-6886-0	302.34	P/780	©2015
How to Deal with an Adult Bully Addy Ferguson • 978-1-4777-6881-5 eBook: 978-1-4777-6883-9	302.34	M/690	©2015
Smartphone Bullying Addy Ferguson • 978-1-4777-6888-4 eBook: 978-1-4777-6890-7	302.34	N/720	©2015
What to Do When You Are Bullied for Being Different Addy Ferguson • 978-1-4777-6892-1 eBook: 978-1-4777-6894-5	302.34	L/660	©2015
What to Do When Your Brother or Sister Is a Bully Addy Ferguson • 978-1-4777-6898-3 eBook: 978-1-4777-6897-6	302.34	M/670	©2015
What to Do When Your Friends Are Bullies Addy Ferguson • 978-1-4777-6877-8 eBook: 978-1-4777-6879-2	302.34	P/810	©2015

TITLE	DEWEY	GRL/LEXILE	©
Are You a Bully? Addy Ferguson • 978-1-4488-9666-0 eBook: 978-1-4488-9905-0 • Interactive eBook: 978-1-4777-0031-0	302.34	J/770	©2013
Bullying with Words Addy Ferguson • 978-1-4488-9670-7 eBook: 978-1-4488-9909-8 • Interactive eBook: 978-1-4777-0035-8	302.34	L/870	©2013
Group Bullying Addy Ferguson • 978-1-4488-9669-1 eBook: 978-1-4488-9908-1 • Interactive eBook: 978-1-4777-0034-1	302.34	M/900	©2013
Online Bullying Addy Ferguson • 978-1-4488-9668-4 eBook: 978-1-4488-9907-4 • Interactive eBook: 978-1-4777-0033-4	302.34	O/950	©2013
What to Do if You Are Bullied Addy Ferguson • 978-1-4488-9665-3 eBook: 978-1-4488-9904-3 • Interactive eBook: 978-1-4777-0030-3	302.34	K/830	©2013

What You Can Do to Stop Bullying

How to Deal with an ADULT BULLY

Addy Ferguson

PowerKiDS press.

New York

Published in 2015 by The Rosen Publishing Group, Inc.
29 East 21st Street, New York, NY 10010

First Edition

Editor: Jennifer Way
Book Design: Erica Clendening and Colleen Bialecki
Book Layout: Andrew Povolny
Photo Research: Katie Stryker

Photo Credits: Cover altrendo images/Stockbyte/Thinkstock; p. 4 tammykayphoto/Shutterstock.com; p. 5 Martine Doucet/E+/Getty Images; p. 6 Wavebreakmedia Ltd/Wavebreak Media/Thinkstock; p. 7 MoMorad/E+/Getty Images; p. 9 Monkey Business Images/Shutterstock.com; p. 10 Olesya Feketa/Shutterstock.com; p. 11 Digital Vision/Photodisc/Thinkstock; p. 12 Imagesbybarbara/E+/Getty Images; p. 13 moodboard/Thinkstock; p. 14 Susanne Walstrom/Getty Images; p. 15 Tetra Images/Getty Images; p. 16 Manley099/E+/Getty Images; p. 19 Lewis J Merrim/Photo Researchers/Getty Images; p. 20 Shalamov/iStock/Thinkstock; p. 21 Petrograd99/iStock/Thinkstock; p. 22 Michaeljung/Shutterstock.com.

Library of Congress Cataloging-in-Publication Data

Ferguson, Addy.
 How to deal with an adult bully / by Addy Ferguson. — First edition.
    pages cm. — (Stand up: bullying prevention)
 Includes index.
 ISBN 978-1-4777-6881-5 (library binding) — ISBN 978-1-4777-6882-2 (pbk.) —
ISBN 978-1-4777-6622-4 (6-pack)
 1. Bullying—Juvenile literature. 2. Children and adults—Juvenile literature. I. Title.
 BF637.B85F4685 2015
 302.34'3—dc23
                                   2013047735

Manufactured in the United States of America

CPSIA Compliance Information: Batch #WS14PK5: For Further Information contact Rosen Publishing, New York, New York at 1-800-237-9932

Contents

What Is Bullying?

Have you ever been pushed or teased repeatedly at school, on the bus, or in your neighborhood? Have you seen these things happening to other people? Repeated **aggressive** behavior by one person or group of people against another person is called bullying.

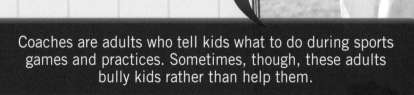

Coaches are adults who tell kids what to do during sports games and practices. Sometimes, though, these adults bully kids rather than help them.

Most often, bullying refers to behavior among school-aged children. Sometimes, though, adults bully children. This can be a very confusing and scary situation for the child being bullied. If an adult is bullying you or someone you know, there are things you can do to get help.

This book will help you tell when an adult's behavior crosses the line into bullying. You will learn what to do if an adult is bullying you or a friend.

Adult Bullying

Most adult bullies bully other adults. Sometimes, adults bully kids, though. A kid might get yelled at if she does something wrong. If an adult uses name-calling or insults, though, he has crossed the line into bullying.

Workplace bullies might be bosses who humiliate the people who work for them because it makes them feel powerful.

Bullies who are kids might taunt or hurt others during recess.

Parents might spank their kids sometimes. This is called **discipline**. Discipline is different from **violence**. No adult other than a parent or guardian should discipline a child physically. No adult should ever use physical violence against a kid. Punching and hitting are violent acts. If an adult says he will hurt you physically, that is a threat. Threats are also bullying.

When Bullying Becomes Abuse

Adults have more power than children. They are bigger and stronger. They are **authority** figures in children's lives. Parents, teachers, relatives, and coaches are all people who have authority in a child's life. Children learn to trust that adults are there to keep them safe.

An adult might bully a child by saying mean, hurtful things about the child. She might threaten to hurt the child if the child does not behave a certain way. When an adult bullies a child, it is a form of **abuse**. Bullying and abuse are wrong.

Teachers are authority figures who are in control of kids' grades. This power can make it scary to speak up when a teacher is bullying kids.

Why Do People Bully?

Sometimes a person bullies others because she likes the feeling of power it gives her. She might think it makes other people like her more, too.

Some bullies may convince their friends to join in with their bullying. They may think that bullying will make them more popular.

Adult bullies sometimes act that way because that is the only way they know how to deal with disagreements.

Other times, the person who bullies feels bad about himself. This person uses bullying to deal with his own low **self-esteem** or **anxiety**. He may also use bullying as a way to fit in with a group of peers. Adults can bully for these reasons, too. Adults who bully children may have been bullied by adults in their past as well. Even if there are reasons for the bullying, it does not make it okay.

How Bullying Hurts

A kid who is being bullied by an adult might think that other adults will only believe the bully. He may have trouble asking for help.

Bullying has lasting effects on the person bullied and the person doing the bullying, too. When an adult bullies a child, it can really hurt that child's self-esteem. That child feels sad, scared, alone, and helpless. When an adult bullies a child, the child may feel that it is his fault. He may feel that other adults will not believe him or care about what is happening.

The helpless feelings caused by bullying can lead to **depression**, anxiety, and low self-esteem. Just remember that not all adults are bullies. A bullied child needs to talk to someone she can trust.

If a kid is being bullied by a teacher at school, she might pretend she is sick so she can stay home and avoid being bullied. This is understandable, but it will not help end the bullying.

Dealing with Adult Bullies

It is never easy to deal with bullying, especially when the bully is an adult. It is important to know that no one deserves to be bullied. If you feel you or someone you know is being bullied, get help! Talk to a friend or trusted adult and ask her to help you make the bullying behavior stop.

Talking to a friend will make you feel better. She also might be able to suggest someone you can talk to about the bullying.

Explain that you are being bullied to a trusted adult. She may decide to meet with the adult who is bullying you and talk about making the bully stop.

With another trusted adult in the room, try to talk to the person doing the bullying. Explain how that adult's behavior is making you feel. Try to come up with new ways for the two of you to communicate that do not resort to bullying.

Stand Up!

Bullying behavior is wrong, but people are often afraid to talk about it. **Bystanders** are the people who see bullying happening and do nothing. They don't want to get involved. This is especially true when kids see an adult doing the bullying. Don't be a bystander. If you or a friend is being bullied, speak out.

Knowing that somebody is paying attention and wants the bullying to stop can make a big difference to the child being bullied. A bullied child feels **isolated** and powerless. If you stand up, she will know she is not alone. This may give her the courage she needs to get help.

A kid who is bullied in front of bystanders may feel especially isolated because he can see that people are doing nothing.

Getting Help from an Adult

It is important to talk to someone, whether you are a witness or a target of bullying. A trusted adult, such as a teacher, guidance **counselor**, or parent, can help you think about ways to stop the bullying. Bullying hurts people, and you should always tell an adult when someone is being hurt.

To stay safe, a child who is being bullied by an adult should have a trusted grown-up with him to talk about the behavior. The adult bully likely needs to seek counseling to stop the behavior. Another adult can offer to help the bully find help.

A kid who has been bullied might visit a counselor to talk about her feelings. Adult bullies should also get counseling to learn how to change their behavior.

Repairing Self-Esteem

It is normal for a person who has been bullied to feel angry, sad, or worried. Do not keep these feelings inside, though. Tell your school guidance counselor or another trusted person your feelings. She can help you see that you have not done anything to deserve being bullied. She can also help you take action.

If you enjoy art, making an art project can help you express your feelings. This is good for your self-esteem.

Writing is a good way to express your feelings. You could try writing out how you would explain to the bully how his actions have made you feel.

Taking action can make you feel like you have control over what is happening. That takes away some of a bully's power. Taking action could mean scheduling a time to talk to the bully with another adult. It could also mean making posters to make other kids aware of this problem.

A Bully-Free Zone

Some schools have programs to make their schools bully-free zones. The whole school works together to make the school a safe place for everyone. The students, teachers, and staff all agree to take action if they see bullying.

You can expand this idea into your community. Have a trusted adult help you talk to town officials about ways to raise awareness about bullying. A bully-free world can exist. It all starts with one person who is willing to take a stand against bullying.

It takes both adults and kids working together to create a bully-free community.

Glossary

abuse (uh-BYOOS) Treating someone in a harmful way.

aggressive (uh-GREH-siv) Ready to fight.

anxiety (ang-ZY-eh-tee) Uneasiness or worry.

authority (uh-THOR-ih-tee) The power to give commands.

bystanders (BY-stan-derz) People who are there while something is taking place but are not taking part in what is happening.

counselor (KOWN-seh-ler) Someone who talks with people about their feelings and problems and who gives advice.

depression (dih-PREH-shun) A sickness in which a person is very sad for a long time.

discipline (DIH-sih-plin) Punishment used to teach proper behavior.

isolated (EYE-suh-layt-ed) Apart and alone.

self-esteem (SELF-uh-STEEM) Happiness with oneself.

violence (VY-lens) Strong force used to cause harm.

Index

A
adult(s), 5–8,
    11–15, 17–18,
    21–22
anxiety, 11, 13

B
bystander(s), 17

C
counselor,
    18, 20

D
depression, 13
discipline, 7

G
guardian, 7

H
help, 5, 14, 17–18

I
insults, 6

N
name-calling, 6

S
self-esteem,
    11–13

T
threat(s), 7

V
violence, 7

Websites

Due to the changing nature of Internet links, PowerKids Press has developed an online list of websites related to the subject of this book. This site is updated regularly. Please use this link to access the list: www.powerkidslinks.com/subp/adult/